PLAYING AT STILLNESS

Playing *at*
STILLNESS

RHINA P. ESPAILLAT

Truman State University Press
New Odyssey Series

Published 2005 by Truman State University Press, Kirksville, Missouri 63501
tsup.truman.edu

Cover photo: George Brawerman
Cover design: Teresa Wheeler
Body type: Adobe Garamond; Adobe Garamond is a registered trademark of Adobe
   Systems Incorporated.
Printed by: Thomson-Shore, Dexter, Michigan USA

Library of Congress Cataloging-in-Publication Data

Espaillat, Rhina P. (Rhina Polonia), 1932–
   Playing at stillness : poems / by Rhina P. Espaillat.
      p. cm. — (New odyssey series)
   ISBN 1-931112-48-7 (alk. paper)
   I. Title. II. Series.
   PS3555.S535P58 2005
   811'.54—dc22

                                                                   2005000143

For Alfred, whose love has shaped the life folded into these poems,
and for our sons, who have linked it to the future.

CONTENTS

WOOL FROM AN OLD SWEATER

ACKNOWLEDGMENTS

I wish to express my thanks to the following publications, in which some of the poems in *Playing at Stillness* first appeared:

Amelia: "Circling the Jellyfish," "The Poet Makes Chicken Soup," "Tea," and "Undelivered Mail"
America: "Counterclockwise" and "Settling"
The American Scholar (Phi Beta Kappa Society): "Needlework"
Bitterroot: "When We Sold the Tent"
Blue Unicorn: "Cousins," "Eden on Sunday," "Martha Considers the Lilies," and "Prime Numbers"
Bronte Street: "Knee Deep in August"
Caprice: "Mission Bell"
Cicada: "Drinking the Colors"
Croton Review: "People in Home Movies"
Freshet: "Compensation"
Galley Sail Review: "Tribute"
Garden Lane: "This Is to Tell You"
Home Planet News: "On the Avenue"
In Other Words: Literature by Latinas of the U.S.: "The Ballad of San Isidro"
Chester H. Jones Foundation National Poetry Competition Chapbook, 1984: "Weeping Fig"
Ladies' Home Journal: "Nativity"
The Lyric: "Back Yard Talk," "Between You and the Dead, It's All Uneven," "Express," "Marginal," "Overheard at the Zoo," "Reading," "Remind Me, Gold," and "Six"
Modern Lyrics Anthology: "Kite Flying"
The Muse Anthology: "Snow"
The New Press: "Woolworth"
The New York Times: "...After the Signal" and "Vandalism"
Parthenon Anthology: "Old House" and "Sad Song"
Phase & Cycle: "Bird Summer" and "Four"
Piedmont Literary Review: "Through the Window" and "The Way Things Are"
Pivot: "Variations on a Theme of May Swenson"

Plains Poetry Journal: "Any Soldier," "Easy Words," "Eyes," "February," "For an Old Friend Encountered Unexpectedly," "Michael's Veterans Remember," "October," "Primitive Landscape," "Raccoon," "Wheelchairs," and "Wild Roses"

Poet Lore: "November Music"

Poetry Digest: "January Buds"

Poetry Review: "Physics"

Slant: "Particles"

Voices International: "Arachne," "Chapter One," "A Eulogy, Maybe," "I Heard You Moving Through the Web of Sleep," "Late January," "Look to the Small Birds," "Morning Song," and "Queen Anne's Lace"

Yankee: "Two Nuns at the Mall"

NUCLEUS TO NEBULA

Weeping Fig

If you have ever wept
we have not seen it,
but only

the tilt of your blind eyes
to the stroke of light,
your sure, deaf

listening to time's bell.
We name you, as we
name, through the

glass of our obsessions,
careless galaxies,
and post there

a legendary guard
circling our fortunes,
our orbits.

As we name Impatiens,
Star of Bethlehem,
and Weeping

Willow, but cannot know
what you name yourselves,
if naming

compels you, or what you
would think—if you thought—
of our noise,

our pale unresting leaves
beating at still air,
our weeping.

Any Soldier

Above the field where summer clings
a blackbird barks his curt command.
He wears his dark fatigues, a band
of campaign ribbons on his wings.

I halt; we parley, eye to eye;
he grants me passage through his weeds
strictly along a path that leads
back to the trail I chose to try.

Civilian to my very core,
I find safe passage and free choice
equal in value, and his voice
repellent as an act of war.

Still, any soldier, I suppose,
however rude, is due some praise
who keeps his post through dwindling days
defending all the ground he knows.

Through the Window

The surface of the pond is curdled silver
above a hemisphere of pebbled blue
in which our trees, inverted, tremble over
which heaven is true.

One leaf launched at the edge fractures the static
mirror with a quick frenzy of unmaking,
and birds plying deep routes waver, erratic,
as if winds were raking.

Idle before the windowsill I stand,
my work undone, to watch reflections jangle
as harp strings may, struck by a casual hand,
see colors wrangle

in happy mock discord. But work is waiting
and must be taken up again: this real
soberly threaded needle, socks for mating,
vegetables to peel.

Life is a serious thing, I tell the pond,
not lightly set aside or left to do
for the mere whimsicalities of one
undisciplined as you.

Look to the Small Birds

If a starved wind
gnaw the woods bare,
look to the small birds gleaning
razor-cold air.

In a fence-cornered haven,
scatter wild seed;
let no swift move frighten
small birds that feed.

Through days that drift like ashes
and nights of stone,
no one who shelters small birds
is quite alone.

Overheard at the Zoo

All morning I've been
balancing junk on my nose
waving both flippers
to please these idiots and where's
the kid with my pail of fish?

Raccoon

We've got you now in the dusty beam that creeps
up the trunk after you, sweeps undersides
of leaves spread hands up like accomplices.
We catch you head down, in a halo.

No bullets, but the camera frisking
you there for your days deep as parables;
blind in our own lightning, we shoot to hold
you, your whisk tail, the twin moons of your gaze.

But it is you who hold us, mystery
blooming this once in our city maple, you
whose dainty fingers close on us like love
and neither take us with you nor let us go.

Queen Anne's Lace

You rise, angelic, from green
meadows where the sun
beats its brass drum and shadows fall
like small change
out of the wind's pockets.

The noonday bird leans earthward
from his cloudy perch,
but you, whose feet are nailed with stones
to the brown
grain of the meadow, you

rise with clean upturned faces,
you levitate on
the scorching breath of summer, white
flightless wings
moving in place like prayer.

Counterclockwise

Some of the world's leading theorists have speculated that if… the universe begins to contract, the arrow of time will change direction.
—Walter Sullivan, *New York Times,* 30 Dec. 1986

Seedlings shudder and
suck themselves down
into the brown that settles to
smooth, and tuck
themselves under.

Seeds lift their heads clear
and wrap themselves
in spilled pulp gathered whole again;
the rind shuts
neatly, seamless.

Then the fruit leaps up
to the thinning
branch, deflates to petaled nodule,
bud, scale, speck,
flattens to bark.

Imploding, the tree
unspins itself
like a voyage told in reverse
to seedling,
seed, fruit, dissolve.

Prime Numbers

If you imagine
that we are heroic in
our asymmetry,

forget that pipe dream:
we did not design ourselves
to be metaphor.

All knees and elbows,
kinks and crannies of conscience,
which of us could make

those compromises
that policy requires
to choose one purpose,

gear to one method
or clench to one fulfillment?
We leave it to the

four and eight to be
predictable, simple dupes;
with pretensions to

wit, nine and fifteen
are equally transparent;
and worst of all, six—

round-heeled peacemaker—
bends its no-spine to all winds,
salutes every flag.

No, we are content
to remain discontented
and digest nothing.

Snow

Deception underfoot,
deception on the bough:
it covers bud and root
to state the naked now

as the full-flowered tree
would charm this out of mind.
All presence seems to be
deception of a kind.

Wild Roses

Between two hillsides, where a spear of silver
cleaves green from green,
I found wild roses blossoming between
boulder and river.

Bright burned each flower with the stream's obsession
to sever and depart—
but for the pull of stone, the long adhesions
like vessels round the heart,

round the divided heart that never knows
which to obey,
those tangled roots that nest it where it grows,
this flowing fall that summons it away.

Back Yard Talk

Nature says resurrection, but I say
there's no such cradle music promised for
the dying tips she snips off, whose live core
we guess at far away.

I try to teach her loss: how vanished leaves,
ambition, friends, cry at the door of faith.
She answers me with spring, as if that wraith
healed everything that grieves.

My brisk old neighbor likes to work alone,
is off about her business. But I find,
some days, trifles like mercy left behind:
odd shells, translucent stone.

When Nature pins the seasons end to end
on the long snapping line she dries them on,
I wonder if she'll notice that I'm gone
and wish we had been friends.

Primitive Landscape

On a plump hillside lush with sheep and children,
solid black birds creak slowly into flight
under the pale blue dome that cups the world.
In flowing ropes of blue the fish are sleeping.
So life might flow season-by-season by,
combed as the crops that velvet these small fields.

I could believe the welcome of these fields
a father's gift to well-deserving children
for their enjoyment and glad rest laid by,
but that I know how early peace takes flight
and other dreams beguile, as we lie sleeping:
illusions, promises this placid world

was never made to keep. Where does that world,
alien to this, unfold its restless fields?
Whose is the voice that taunts us, as we, sleeping,
moan, tossing in our nakedness, like children
trapped in our wingless hungering for flight
as all we loved makes haste to pass us by?

Hold to this quiet scene, comforted by
a rapt, horizonless, four-sided world
in which light falls like justice, and the flight
of hours takes nothing from unaltered fields,
nothing from the allegiance of these children
whose life is flowing while their souls are sleeping.

But look: in this bird's eye something is sleeping
venomous as a sneer: unsweetened by
the smooth, orderly singing of the children

it coils upon itself to hiss the world,
tip the full urn of sorrow on these fields,
sour the crops unpicked and put to flight

the innocence of streams. Perhaps no flight
can happen till the heart is raked from sleeping
by dark, disordered hopes that make the fields
shiver as if chill winds were whistling by.
Perhaps we were not meant to love a world
that fattens us for death, like greedy children.

I wrench myself to flight, not quite seduced by
this charmed ground held sleeping from the world,
homeward to bleaker fields and sadder children.

Bird Summer

This was the summer of the fallen bird—
swallow or swift—we found hunched in the grass
trailing one wing outstretched like a gray fan.

In the makeshift nest of my cupped hand, it drank
sugar water slow-squeezed out of a dropper
into the yellow gape of its beak.

All day, talons and all, it warmed my palm;
by night, comic and fierce and sad, its small
fixed stare froze in its eyes, and it lay still.

Afterward I thought of eagles, angels,
annunciations, and the crest of Caesar:
history's hindsight, the tarnish of thought.

Bird is what this summer taught my flesh:
black unreadable eyes, intimate, alien
pulse against my pulse like a feathered watch.

Physics

Filter me like rain
nucleus to nebula, forever;
grant me safe-conduct
everywhere, like sand.
Comfort my losses
with convergences:
promise me the sun's
ashes in my bones,
curl the tides of my blood
around the moon,
pen the sea
behind the fretwork of my eyelids.
Teach me to cherish
what is
more than the law that names it;
sustain me as I loosen
the straps of appearance and let go.
Bequeath me my father, who
shrugged off the skin of his half life
and went home
like a dying star.

Particles

Sun cannot follow us into the rough white
flesh of clouds we pierce like a winged scalpel.
We cut into shadow, into the pocket
of our made horizon, comfortably slanted

over water shifting its blue scales;
we slide landward, a little sick with descent.
Lit strands of the city tilt up to
tangle us in the human element.

And there they pass through us—neutrinos, those
travelers from ports beyond our knowing—
to fly on into stone, the planet's body
all open lanes to their soundless going.

Maudslay Park

The riverbank and its reflection move
downstream together, one stirred by wind
but steady in its tangle of boughs and patches
of fading light, one jangled by current,
trembling like the strings of a struck harp.

Or, rather, neither moves; only the flat
scales of the river jostle and tilt their way
seaward forever, slowing, reluctant
there at the shallows, dividing and shearing
into coils that stream away around rock snouts.

The riverbank rises; candlestick trees
lit by late sun shelter the last cold birds.
Its reflection dives into another blue
with steel in it, cobalt and mercury;
there the boughs are made and unmade without end.

Above us, beyond the pocket our breath inhabits,
light gives way: unimaginable black
as far as thought will go, and farther.
Beneath us, dark millstones drag the continents
gritty, agonized inches through drowned bones.

Standing beside this shore, we are all moving—
we, the trees, the solid metallic river—
all particles twirling, rebounding, thinnest cloud
peppered by a rain of electric sky-dust
that needles through the planet with one stitch.

But at this moment, caught in a web of motion
we play at stillness, imagine ourselves
imagining the sun, the riverbank
and its reflection, behind us the cries
of gulls and children, the voices of friends.

HOME MOVIES

Eden on Sunday

"Thinking in prose," I tease him, "you've all but
come full circle round, the way you creep
reason to reason, where my instincts leap
at once, with both eyes shut."

the comfort-littered room is warm and dry,
snug as a bathysphere against the rain
whose thousand fingers tapping on the pane
are mutinous and sly.

We trade newspapers, pausing now and then
to argue politics and share fresh fruit.
Bound to the word, his eyes ride sure and mute
sideways and back again.

Something in me is restless with the slow
pursuit of purposes, however just;
wants to set out on roads I nearly trust
where reason will not go.

Something in me is fearless of the night,
as if in league with the wild thing out there
that must invade this bubble of closed air,
challenge this quiet light.

Mine is a yearning rustle of lost wings
beating to foolishness, perhaps, or song;
his, the untangling of the least thread wrong
in the tight web of things.

Locked in his wistful faith, as in live stone,
we're sheltered from the truth he calls mistakes.
"Thinking in prose," I tell him, sighing, "makes
odd music of its own."

Circling the Jellyfish

When they walk the beach
barefoot, trailing their separate
urgencies, hers are the slow tracks
that circle the jellyfish.
His vanish into foam.

"Hurry up," he says,
leaning on sea wind toward places
where the view has to be better.
But she is riveted to
this glassy wafer,

watery daisy,
blind eye straining to blink, dazzled
by so much sun. And she measures
the distance between heaven
and dying earthbound.

"Don't touch it," he shouts:
but she is trying with one foot
to flip it home, to tip it free
of seawrack and bottlecaps.
He calls her away.

All afternoon, through
the sweet stink of indifferent
prodigality, cool salty
sea tang flavored with murder
and the slime of birth,

he skims horizons.
But she bends over breathing holes
sucking themselves into wet sand
where the tide draws its white scarf
carefully away.

She is kneeling to
what lives there, what is extending
itself, translucent and fragile,
under the pound and whisper
of beating water.

Everything is bruised:
mussel shells on crooked hinges
that neither fold again to pray
nor unfold to fly; crab claws
flimsy as cheap toys.

Mourning for the void,
he inscribes blue spaces above
the sea's chorus of small hungers,
the clutter of broken things;
but she is bruised by

she is anchored by
the look of life's empty cages.
She is circling the jellyfish,
loyal as the womb; she is
mourning Genesis.

Kite Flying

Looped to my children's hands,
a painted star.
They'll reel it in by and by,
from up so far

I can't be sure I see it.
How do they know
the sky will give them back
what they let go?

Around them as they move
the air is bright:
they make the morning come
and bless the night.

When at my loving's tether
they pull and fling,
where shall I find the courage
to pay out string?

Learning to Ride

Grounded in childhood by my mother's fear,
I swallow down my own, ignore the snide
whispered amusement of the cackling gear,
grip both rubber-tipped horns, and learn to ride.

Crisscrossed against my will, I hang on, clenched
grim as teeth on this perverse machine
that mangles pride and ankles; weary, drenched
with pulling out of falling, wheel again,

deaf to old cautions, fueled by some need
more vital than whole bones. Sudden as fire,
miraculous, I balance, water, and feed
all my lost hopes on this absurd desire;

I fly above the wind who never ran,
and round and round the speeding streets go past,
circling my fifty years, the careful man
whose watching eyes tether me home at last.

For My Son on His Wedding Day

In your fisherman's room, becalmed by loss,
I sit, thinking Yes hard while the heart cries No
whose love you landed, unfished-for, long ago.
Mother, pet nag, Blue Fairy, and albatross,
truer than any compass, stubborn as whale,
I cursed you with gloves and lunches and beliefs,
harpooned you with Don'ts, dragged anchor to your sail,
and, whether wrong or unforgivably right,
sighted everywhere storms and secret reefs.
Now, beached as the tide goes out that bears away
both the man and the boy you were, what can I say?
That fear is the fare we pay to all delight;
that none steer blithely with so much to lose;
that if I doled out like rations your right to choose,
I flung out by prodigal handfuls joy to your joy,
balm to your grief; that, proud of my tall, fair boy,
I wish you, too, beautiful sons and daughters,
and long, miraculous fishing in quiet waters.

October

Under the willows
I take my mother walking.
Gold leaves are waving

and the first wild geese
pour southward down the clear blue
sluices of heaven.

The wind is turning
chill; my mother is cautious,
her hand on my arm.

Reflected in her
eyes, ducks on the pond sail by,
trailing silver wakes.

No more cicadas;
their iridescent prisons
hang on the tall reeds.

In the willows, in
my mother's slow joy, something
is waving goodbye.

The Trap

Safe in my purse, Ilana Beth—
my granddaughter—is caught mid-breath
with furrowed brow, on Mama's lap.
One hand is raised as if to clap
zen-style, and her stern gaze pursues
her fingers, as if asking "Whose?"

She doesn't know her hands, her shoes,
her features in the glass, her name.
Or did not, for this moment came
and went, as moments do, and now
I'm told she knows the what and how
of her small person to a T.

But in my purse she stays the same,
her last year's photo crammed beside
her great-grandfather's, who died
decades ago, and here—come see—
the boy her father used to be.

This is the comfort-baited trap
that we slip into as we age:
the book falls open to one page
whose plot we like, or lack thereof.
We shelve the sequel, call it love,
and live suspended in midair
above the climate love should bear.

Ilana Beth, I promise you
the hardest work the old can do
I'll do, for your most precious sake:

I promise you to stay awake
through all the changes you must make,
however breathlessly you run,
and bring no memories to cage
what you must do with what you've done,
no yellowed photographs to curse
your passage out of every purse.

Six

Evan is angry;
God knows why.
Perhaps his mother, the despot,
has made him cry
insisting on dinner now,
not by and by.

Perhaps his father, the bully,
has had the gall
to summon him for a bath.
he kicks the wall,

waves Grandpa off with one
translucent fist.
There's his chicken untouched,
Grandma unkissed,

bedtime story unread.
Upstairs he cocks his thumb
and aims one lethal finger:
now let them come!

Four

Her job is curing
whatever her brother kills
with his plastic sword.

She does it with fruit—
wax bananas, grapes, apples—
spoonfed to lumpy

faded casualties.
She does it quickly, keeping
pace with the carnage,

but confidently,
as one sure of miracles,
the power of food,

her firm hand wielding
a spoon not too badly bent,
a sense of mission.

Cousins

We share cheekbones, a curve of the mouth,
or the head thrown back at just such an angle
to laugh; ferns laugh in the sun at the graves
we visit, mosses cradle in our names.

"Look, we are what became of you," we say
to our dead, "we are the streams you flow in
after the eddies, the purling of will
and accident, the small permutations.

Our gestures conjugate you, pass your one
dictum forward in a change of tense,
echo your gospel without end, like
a field of grass turning the way the wind goes."

But the dead never answer; we cannot know,
when we branch away into the future, just what
they make of us wearing ourselves like clothes
to cover the naked singleness they left us.

Drinking the Colors

She turns to ask me
Will I drink all these colors
And Yes I tell her

It's water does that   she says
and points to the stone fences

Yes I say   We walk
the landscape of October
she hanging heavy

on the bones of my bent arm
A long cry caught in my throat

She turns to ask me
Am I really her daughter
And Yes I stroke her

And Yes the trees are weeping
and we drinking under them

This Is To Tell You

This is to tell you that your silver's gone
to one granddaughter, and the other's taken
the china that you said was much too fine
to serve on, which perhaps will not be broken
in transit. Neighbors, come to pay their last
respects, went home with armfuls: your good glasses,
blankets, sheets you grew frail on, and those best
slips you were saving for forgotten dresses.

The heavy-lidded pot in which you conjured
your sacramental chicken, your brown stew
ambrosial with onions, I took home, whom your
firstborn took home to you decades ago,
when you were bent with fruit, a summer bough,
and I was half the age my son is now.

Instruction

He wants to show me
which is the key that will keep
me warm   how the lock

works that will shut out
the silence always waiting
there for his absence

He wants me to learn
what forms to fill out after
the end of the world

where to apply for
the rest of my life   But I
hide my eyes   my ears

I Heard You Moving
Through the Web of Sleep

I heard you moving through the web of sleep
and improvised a dream—a thread of plot
as plausible as most, I guess—to keep
from following you out into the not-
yet-morning half-light of real time. You were,
I think, alone, climbing a grassy hill,
or seated on it, stroking the green fur
of its round back, looking away, quite still.
And something in that scene, or in your calm
impersonal regard, so harrowed me
that sleep was shattered as by some alarm
shrieking inside my head to wake and see
(But what was there to see or understand?)
if that live warmth was you beneath my hand.

Tribute

Earth, this is Frinkus: now into your keeping
accept him, his few shaggy pounds of leaping
small bones, high treble bark, and doting eyes.

He hectors neighbors' hounds eight times his size
and comes to you replete with minor crimes:
author of secret puddles, he sometimes
duns us at meals for dainty bits to eat.

He likes his belly rubbed by Papa's feet,
and has a trick of spinning in mid-air
that makes him seem a shuttlecock of hair.

Love's absence is his hell; his only notion
of heaven, love's return. He thinks devotion
a joy that only death can take away.
May half as much be said for us one day.

Needlework

Today I am her
sister   She tells me again
how proud she is of

my careful cutting   my neat
seams   She pats my folded hands

You have silky skin
just like my daughter   she says
I miss her these days

Look   I tell her   here I am
Your one daughter   Your one child

So you are   she laughs
and claps her hands   Your father
was here this morning

I picture my father's bones
perched cross-legged on her bed

and smile   She strokes my
cheek   You have my daughter's smile
she says   I miss her

these days   And goes on to speak
of our mother's small stitching

People in Home Movies

People in home movies are always turning
or lurching too close, passing through and out
of focus, big bleared faces all patches
and shards of color; we want to tell them,
"Stop! Hold still a while against that background
of shifting leaves and water." But they keep moving

over the edge, like doomed sailors, moving
too fast for any lens, their backs turning
as the film twitches over sky, gates, ground,
anonymous pastures, a road splayed out,
looped in again. By now we've lost them,
their absence as disfiguring as patches.

Memory, at our age, is bits and patches:
Whose faces were those? Where were they, moving
under those blurred clouds, laughing? Behind them,
what sea was that, and when did all that turning
foam unfold itself over the sand and out
again? Names, features, fragments litter the ground

we flicker across, as in a burial ground,
graves of old friends standing out like patches.
We know who they were, but time rubs out
the writing, and the camera moving
through past weathers is too hurried, turning
our sudden decades too close to save them.

We would need to reel backward to pursue them,
make ourselves as we were, strip from the ground
these crops coaxed from ourselves by the turning

of each sun, back to bare soil and patches
of early light, before God's rain moving
among small roots woke us and tricked us out.

And would it be worth it, after all, out
of a moment's regret, to run toward them
and buy them back at the price of ourselves, moving
weightless out of ourselves into heart's ground,
the future discarded like old clothes full of patches,
and the child in us naked, dancing and turning?

People in home movies want out: they hide underground
or behind new faces that cover them like patches;
they age, they change, they keep moving past all returning.

THE WAY THINGS ARE

Easy Words

Where do they go, those cruel, those easy words
we wield in haste and toss away like knives?
Do they flap back to peck at us, fat birds
fed on our long regretting all our lives?

Do they bloom out in waves that shear the sky,
ever-unfolding fan of living blade,
so that no gift of balm can rocket by,
outdistancing to heal the hurt once made?

Or do they burrow inward through the soul,
borrowing justice from the lack of light,
and, breeding reasons in that self-sealed hole,
contrive to sleep, content that right makes right?

Where do they go, the casual wounds we say
by nothing made, that nothing takes away?

A Eulogy, Maybe

Nobody praises pigeons. Of course the dove,
symbolic snow or silver aglow in myth,
begetter of gods, like the swan, is another story.
Even the sparrow earns a kind of glory
street-fighting for his bread, tough, resolute,
evasive and trim in his practical city brown.
But he lives under and above, not with
the human neighbors with whom he shares the town,
just out of reach, nowhere and everywhere.
Swallow and jay,
blackbird in his fashionable suit,
beguile us in passing. Sometimes transfigured air
shimmers with some exotic guest
or echoes with a call
too far, too wild for any nest.
We bend with longing, the secret homage of
something in us that wants to fly away.

But pigeons, too plump for glamour, circumspect,
must settle for a crumb
of scant affection, no respect at all.
And still, they come.
Assuming welcome, they turn up in a bunch
like relatives; relentless, they find us
in our solitude, and stay for lunch.
Mostly earthbound,
like us, their conversation's not select.
They strut for hours, mutter old news
and make the most of any common ground.
Fulfilled by sidewalks and by vagrants' shoes,

they have no interest in the rare or far,
and stoop for our stale bread, as to remind us
of who and what and why and where we are.

Nativity

How shall I fashion for my boy
the marvel of that winter night?
His reason shall deny its joy,
my very breath blow out the light;

and still that haloed head, absurd
as winged children treading sky,
is truer than the seen and heard
within whose nets we daily die.

Eyes

His jeweled head ablaze with eyes, the fly
moves in a wilderness of day
in which he sees all things and finds them good.
Tentative as a sage, he makes his way
by indirection and oblique retreats.
Prince of the air, philosopher, he eats
droppings and honey, savoring both the same.
Would I trade places with him if I could?

Picture the shining bubble
in which my youth was spent, those flying hours
measuring stars and flowers,
reading God's name
with twenty-twenty sight!
Now I put down one half of my four eyes
and rub the other two: round each pale letter
crawls its shimmering double.
There's something to be said for any fly's
three-hundred-sixty full, flawless degrees
of familiarity with all he sees.

And still,
there's something paralyzing to the will
in all that vision. Better,
perhaps—Thoreau said "Simplify"—
a single eye.

What concentration! Solid as a chain,
each glance would wed the cyclops to his goal.
No double images, no astigmatic
hints of a world behind the world, no soul.

The man of action, never rendered static
by scruple or sophisticate's disdain
for what he sees, sees only what is there:
that's all he knows.
Sometimes I wish I had his knack
for forward motion with no looking back…

But I don't like the way his story goes:
tricked by that fiend Ulysses and his crew,
blubbering by the sea in blind despair,
he makes the fly seem lucky. Perhaps two
eyes are safest, since we seem not meant
to move in too much light
or be too wise or certain or content.

Two Nuns at the Mall

Black and white and black, they fall upstairs
to Better Dresses, where I spot them later
fingering cocktail silks. The short one wears

wire rims like a double yoke; the taller one
wears amber freckles whose color comes and goes.
They are still young; they laugh in unison

discreetly through Lingerie and up a flight
past Furs and Leather, Domestics and Layettes
and out of sight, all white and black and white.

For an Old Friend
Encountered Unexpectedly

Is this you, dangling on a silver cross
tangled in curls beneath a shopper's ear?
See how your playful twin turns as she moves,
dances, twinkling. I looked for you last year

in Old Jerusalem, but found your place
taken; you were nowhere in sight to drive
away the merchants who festoon their goods
along the street death crowned you on. Alive—

so said your message in the olive garden—
even at the grave you walked away from
you would not flesh out my wish, although my prayer
built you a creche and my need begged you to come.

Now here you are, unsought, private, a tiny
brightness in the supermarket line;
a stranger wears you crucified above
the bread and beer she separates from mine.

You gods are your own masters, come and go
not as we will but as you will, unfound
by any grace of ours, who never know
when light will break or where is holy ground.

Answering to Rilke

Cramped by this indoor season—it's beginning
to feel as if winter will never go—
I chafe at my clutter of things, the flotsam gathered
around me like moss on a stone. "You must change
your life," says Rilke: and I say, Good;
let's start by simplifying, by tossing out.

Here's my wedding gown (when was I this thin?) out
of style, touched by mildew. A hard beginning!
Well, Rainer Maria, must I make good
on my vow to pry myself loose, let go,
"travel light," as the priesthood does, risk change?
Look how the sleeves are puffed, the waist gathered,

the neckline prim for our families gathered
to watch us spin a thread and send it out
into a common future. How people change
to braid into one, how such a beginning
dances into mystery! This must go
back into folded tissue, still mine, still good.

These are some books I meant to read a good
forty years ago. Still waiting, gathered
in dust, in silence. Each feels like a map. Go
find the girl who chose them? No, she's out
of print. But open one, smell: a beginning,
a beckoning route, that paper challenge to change.

Here, put them back: they salvage, safe from change,
read or unread, what was perhaps most good
in her, as she was at our beginning.

And look, my father's foreign coins, gathered
in lieu of travel: how toss them out?
Let them bear witness that he meant to go.

Old yellowed invitations: did I go?
Early pictures of people beyond change,
buried, estranged, divorced: childhood will out.
And in the requisite blue ribbon—Good
grief!—love letters long forgotten, gathered
to celebrate even a false beginning.

Nothing to go, Rilke. Maybe it's good
for change to surprise us in the mess we've gathered.
Figuring out that much is a beginning.

Compensation

My neighbor listens hard to cross the street,
feels for our bell and then for me, a pan
of fresh-baked cake in her free hand. I can
taste with my eyes, as she cannot, the sweet
clumps of half-melted chocolate. Careful feet
remembering which way the floorboards ran,
she smiles at my full vase, tilting a fan
of fingers round it; stoops to find a seat.

This compensation, she says, is simply what
she has to learn before the darkness closes
wholly; and I think, How expensive to be taught
out of such loss to harvest partial good,
the spicy, damp topography of roses,
birdsong, a neighbor's cheek, the grain of wood.

Mission Bell

The priest at that time traded ten of the village children
to slavers in exchange for this bell.
—Native American guide, Acoma Pueblo, New Mexico, 1988

Did you transform their
cries in dry desert silence
into litanies

in praise of Jesus?
Did you stop their mothers' ears
with hymns to Mary?

Priest, did you weigh them
against this heavy brazen
tongue tolling God's love?

Express

The stranger on my left has closed his eyes;
his earphones lock him in their small embrace
away from me. Another stranger lies
sprawled across the aisle, his stony face
daring my look to find him. On my right
a stranger in white uniform observes
each motion of my hand, her purse clutched tight.
We touch from time to time rounding the curves,
but look away, murmuring indistinct
apologies. And yet we wear the one
flesh garment on our bones, must all be linked,
made of the same old spillage from the sun,
born of that first combustion in the dark
once, when the constellations were a spark.

Martha Considers the Lilies

Dancing above the field, they play the field,
unmindful of dark stems whose one desire
anchors them to the earth. Roots' work concealed
by summer green, they levitate, on fire
with nothing but the sun, as if to say,
"We need not spin the glory that we wear
unearned; it spins—it sings—itself." And they
rebuke us in the prison of our care.
But they are not the field: the field is hard
and angular with stones, and yields no bloom
unless desire burrows past earth's guard
while each seed labors to prepare a room.
Labor's the truth that makes us more than free:
dancing above the field is fantasy.

Reading

My name has been called
before a roomful of
waiting strangers:

too late to be dead,
fall downstairs, disappear,
or change my name.

They are listening
for the jingle of my
keys to open

those other places.
How shall I confess my
empty pockets?

What will they do when
I hold up my naked
voice to their need,

when they smell my days
out loud in every line
like crushed garlic?

They'll know I've never
chained the sea, talked back to
God, been outside

old habits I wear
like arch supports; they will
call the police.

Michael's Veterans Remember

We saw them hacked from glory, saw them driven
like leaves November-tossed, their golden ranks
bleeding along the dark that circles Heaven;
mercy was never asked, and never given.
Later we laid our armor down, gave thanks.

Innocent as we were, we had not thought
a father's love transient as credit bought
with iron fealty. Dreadful, the flashes
of His strange reason searing all or naught;
dreadful, the taste of right bitter with ashes.

Our brothers' pride, like innocence, cast out
by Him whose majesty must shape our days,
we sing against the counterpoint of doubt
whining in our ears, and bless His ways
with loud, uneasy praise and praise and praise.

The Way Things Are

This poem wants to be about
the way things are,
but it doesn't know how.

It set out to interview God,
but first bungled the questions
and then the answers.

It came home with
carrots and radishes instead;
it likes the way I handle a paring knife.

It believes the reversed
curves of red peppers
intricate as print

sheltering the small white
sense of seeds;
it respects the terse way olives

punctuate these green meanderings
of lettuce. Yes, it can see
there are urgencies like creditors

pressing hard on the kitchen window;
no, its judgment is not reliable;
no, it is not afraid

or ashamed to have squandered
twenty-four lines
on the contents of this dish.

Wheelchairs

Arrayed as if this ward were some bright deck
scrubbed for a long, romantic, costly cruise,
they wait for passengers, steel arm and neck
gleaming with welcome. Three, exchanging views,
huddle like cronies glad to be aboard
together among strangers; here and there
a loner muses; two lean close to hoard
some gossip much too scandalous to share.

Nurses in soft pastels chatter and smile;
light music tinkles somewhere overhead,
and floral paintings in a sprightly style
conjure the ghost of summer, long since dead.
But wheelchairs, glinting, wink as if to say,
"Not now, not yet, but you and I, someday..."

On the Avenue

I said to God (It was a windy day
and we were waiting for the light to change
on Fifty-ninth Street, where black coaches wait
for tourists, and dejected horses pay
little attention to the passing scene)
I said to God, "Look at these creatures: fate—
that is, Your will—stranded them on the dung
heap of this life. I'm sure You could arrange
something more suited to their speed and grace
than midtown tours and lunch out of a bag.
And while I have Your ear..."
        (The light was green
and we strolled on, The Plaza on our right,
and on our left, breakdancers)
        "...that gray hag
there, with her entourage of pigeons, face
like a map of madness, ankles blue
with body's riot thick in every vein,
is this what living earns, is this Your view
of what old age deserves? That boy, delight
miraculous in every move, performs
for shifting crowds, and having danced and sung
his hours away, scoops up his change and moves
along. Is this Your plan for us, the end
of miracles?
        I tell you as a friend,
but there are those who say the cosmos proves
You have grown callous to our sort of pain
and have, perhaps, forgot Your own. Or worse,
never did know the fleeting thing that warms
us wearers of flesh, and rule us from above

without the common hurt that couches love.
This is no way to run a universe."

God mulled His answer as we ambled south
in silence, past the shops, Bendel to Saks,
and then He turned to face me, and His mouth
released a spate of starlings, and a peal
of bells, and tiers of dressy shoes, and stacks
of books on sale at Doubleday, and rows
of steaming carts with shish kebabs, meat pies
and every meretricious face The Good
has ever worn.
        Ah, slippery old eel,
I thought, and laughed, what politician knows
how to embroider pseudo-argument
out of non sequiturs like You?
        We should
be angry with You: Oh, the friends You take
like books borrowed forever, laws You make
and fail to keep, injuries You invent
to justify returning each sad prayer
to us unopened! But what's friendship for
if not forgiveness?
        So I let it pass,
indulged Him as He uttered fountains, grass,
Johann Sebastian on steel drums, and more
genial evasions.
        We resumed our walk,
trading impressions through the darkening air,
to the amusement of some two or three
who, disbelieving what the eye can't see,

missed God in the clear robe of His disguise
and, skeptical of solitary talk,
enjoyed my gestures, thinking me alone
above those skaters on their lake of stone.

January Buds

Will they be waiting when I go,
lost boys and girls I used to know?

For so He promised, but I doubt
eyes closed so long will pick me out

under these decades of disguise.
Still, after night the sun does rise

to lend each leaf its proper green.
Let me forget what decades mean,

forgive the promise—kept, unkept—
and leave these empty graves unwept.

Here are the crypts they stagger from:
I will be waiting when they come.

SETTLING

Chapter One

Sleep was all I wanted
but somebody's blood cried Hurry
Hurry the sun is waiting.

So I fell into breath
and daylight, uncoiled like a fern,
learned other voices, although

I was all I wanted—
fingers, mouth, and the tepid sweet
flow I surrounded—and soon

everything exploded:
streets and snowflakes, knees and dog's eyes,
bells and colors and clapping.

To find what I wanted
in that full dish needed both hands,
but the Don'ts snapped like handcuffs

to teach me the shape of
my wrist bones. Time opened and closed,
and my first face slipped away.

Late January

This day gone soft with caving snows
is plotting April underfoot,
but all the promise winter shows
is a dark tracery like soot.

Who can believe in green that comes
borne by a pulse that scarcely beats,
as muffled as defeated drums?
A sky the color of worn sheets,

A sun subdued as final words
is mourning over naked limbs,
weighting the wings of little birds
that skim wide silences like hymns.

The Poet Makes Chicken Soup

What good are you as metaphor? You don't
fly or nest, or sing like a bird, not really;
you strut and stagger, peer one-eyed, scratch, hunt
for grain while the light lasts, comment shrilly

on every barnyard crisis. Cloudburst, dog,
egg and farmer's daughter are all the same
in your vernacular. Tied by one leg
to the pump, one day you shriek for the last time.

Now, metamorphosis: at last we love you,
clear golden gospel we never bothered
to read; intimate as wine, we believe you,
who were never quite plausible when feathered.

Morning Song

Falling back into daybreak
out of dream places,
whom should I meet but memory
wearing my faces:

Wearing the clumsy girl
and the clean bride,
and the listening child
who lives inside,

Wearing the one who broods
and the one who sings,
and the diamond-hard stranger
outside of things,

And the glad woman ragged
with busy giving,
all tumbling out of their lives
into my living.

Oh, what a slow fall, sifting
out of lost places,
gathering down to daybreak
with all those faces!

February

Cold in the pewter sky,
a wet wind crying:
somewhere—elsewhere—
wild geese are flying.

Cold over iron fields,
pale sun is breaking:
under the sleep of stones,
something is waking.

Old House

Old house where I ceased to live, where I live forever
caught as in amber, trapped as the dead remember,
wearing my father's death and my mother's hunger
like a coat made over,

strip it away: I am tired of piety. Sever
the long tight bloodlines from weaver to weaver
unbroken, from giver to giver.
Peel away anger

borne in the bones like death; let me discover
the small bright coin of myself in the purse of some other.
Old house where I never lived, where I die forever,
let it be over.

Knee Deep in August

Knee deep in August, picking what grows
after much coaxing, keeping the bugs away,
the weeds away, I picture a veil of snow
across a winter day.

No sweet red peppers then, filling the dish
with summer and bewildered ants, no more
sweet breasts of grapes to eat unwashed:
winter is all before

and after, either hope or abstinence.
And I remember, with a grateful twinge,
slow days are coming on whose recompense
sings like a rusty hinge

and shuts us in to contemplate year's end
through double windows, to nap, to rearrange
old photographs in albums, to make friends
with what we cannot change.

Undelivered Mail

Dear Daughter,
          Your father and I wish to commend you
on the wisdom of your choices
and the flawless conduct of your life

Dear Poet!
          Where is the full-length manuscript
you promised us? Your check is waiting
The presses are ready
and bookstores are clamoring for delivery

Darling,
          This convention is tedious
beyond belief: the hotel is swarming
with disgustingly overexposed women
far too young to have dignity
or any minds at all

Dear Patient:
          This results of your blood tests reveal
that your problem stems from
a diet dangerously low
in pizza and chocolate

Dear Mom,
          You were right about everything
and I was an idiot not to listen

Remind Me, Gold

I think they're burning leaves beside the lot.
The smell hangs in the air whose honeyed flow
above the last chrysanthemums says autumn;
I'd watch, if I could bring myself to go.

One ought to want the leafless days that come,
as they must come, to put the year to sleep,
but something perverse will hold the passing thing
always a shade more dear than what we keep.

Remind me, gold that settles everywhere,
to prize you when I mourn the bud that broke,
and find in your small secret dust the cure
for summer days gone in a wisp of smoke.

Variations on a Theme of May Swenson

When my long lease is
canceled and I sulk back to
my Father's dark house

What shall I be with
no more rough and smooth of stones,
leaf green, water's kiss

Where shall I pasture
mind's ghost without words, all those
singing fields of runes

Whom shall I follow
on the soft paws of my heart
with human love gone

When We Sold the Tent

When we sold the tent
we threw in the Grand Canyon
with its shawl of pines,
lap full of cones and chipmunks
and crooked seams of river.

We let them have the
parched white moonscapes of Utah,
and Colorado's
magnificat of flowers
sunbursting hill after hill.

Long gentle stretches
of Wyoming, rain outside
some sad Idaho
town where the children, giddy
with strange places, clowned all night.

Eyes like small veiled moons
circling our single light, sleek
shadows with pawprints,
all went with the outfit; and
youth, a river of campfires.

Retrospect

The glass held high before us lets us see
behind us, where remember does its turns.
Things never are the way they used to be.

Wielding the sword of vision, memory
pierces the vanished moment as it burns;
the glass held high before us lets us see,

echoing backward in stern symmetry,
the logic of our seeming. Something yearns
for things less dear the way they used to be,

but, pitiless as God, reveals all three:
the seen, the seer, and the truth he spurns.
The glass held high before us lets us see

the rage we live by, the dichotomy
love trembles at that grieves as it discerns.
Things could not be the way they used to be,

or time, shocked still, pinned as by ecstasy,
would have preserved the light that Plato mourns.
The glass held high before us lets us see
things never were the way they used to be.

November Music

This house contains
me, as my weathered
flesh cradles the loves I breathe.

In basket and vase,
in dusty bowls lie gathered
my smooth

old joys, tame
as the calendar, quietly withered
selves, the face of death

gentled with use, made
sweet, like music; hopes I feathered
for distance with a kind of faith

home here like rain,
and sons I mothered
mirror this place, this life, this man, this mouth.

Settling

When silence
invites each thing to
speak its own name

When darkness
opens every door
where no doors are

I listen
to quiet breakage
the house sighing

lapsing from
plumb lines earthward to
some deeper true

Vandalism

Somebody has stitched
two small black buttons between
my thinning lashes
knotted up at the corners
into untidy gathers.

Somebody has spilled
colorless splotches onto
the roots of my hair,
turned the ends of my mouth down
to quote and unquote my chin.

Somebody has carved
annual rings around my neck,
forged time's signature
on my flesh to make it seem
as if I were growing old.

Sad Song

When I was young of limb,
heart-whole and spry,
no one could pitch a hope
farther than I.

It was no to the halfway thing,
no to the spent,
no to the slow and measured,
the botched and bent.

Now that birdsong is seldom
and the sky less blue,
it's yes to the better than…
and the making do;

yes to the elsewhere eyes
and the sideways kiss.
There is no sad song
sadder than this.

Between You and the Dead,
It's All Uneven

Between you and the dead, it's all uneven:
the more you draw them close to make them bless,
they more they turn away into their haven.

But drive them off, and they will not be driven,
for all your bitter justice and distress.
Between you and the dead lie charges proven

that keep you poised above the hell and heaven
of memory, where there is no redress.
The more they turn away into their leaving,

the more you bind them back; the more they leaven
your nights with stale repentances, the less
between you and the dead that could be loving.

They are beyond the look of faces graven
with sorrows of their making: they are grass,
their turning is no more than Earth revolving.

It is your cry you hear, you are the coven
chanting to raise them. You must let them pass.
You and the dead too long, too long have striven:
They will not turn to bless you unforgiven.

Arachne

Aging, the mind contracts
and learns to do with less:
out of itself exacts
a filament, a tress

to trap the lightest prize,
a joy too fine for sense,
that passion would despise
but for its impotence.

Tea

After the sun has slipped behind the steep
rim of the west, and the last birds are dumb;
after ambition, like the daily hum
of living places, has been put to sleep;
after remembered losses coffered deep
in the heart's tides are stirred to surface from
the dark, are lost again, again to come,
we learn nothing of ours is ours to keep.

How doubly sweet, the haven of this room
bright with the shining trace of what remains
unclaimed by time, unshattered by the sea:
my good companion, walls against the gloom,
young loves like lamps beside the darkening panes,
my fingers warm around this cup of tea.

WOOL FROM AN OLD SWEATER

Marginal

Like the poor everywhere,
the poem lives, if it lives,
by wit and pluck.

It looks over the trash
put out by the five senses—
those rich neighbors—

and uses what it can
like wool from an old sweater.
It warms itself

by dancing, amuses
the crowds waiting in line for
movie tickets.

It walks against the wind,
thinking of summer, teaching
itself to sing.

"…After the Signal"

Listen
Play this tape twice
because all the details
are crucial
I'm calling from
a phone booth
outside Poughkeepsie
with my last
fistful of change
to tell you
that unless the

The Ballad of San Isidro

In the village of San Isidro
they are gathered for a death.
A widow has called for her only son
and begs with her failing breath:

"I have promised you to God, my boy;
oppose me not in this.
Renounce the flesh and serve the Cross
and earn my parting kiss."

Shaken body and soul, he hears
his mother's final prayer,
for body and soul and heart are bound
to a maiden's raven hair,

to a maiden's lips like a honeyed rose
and hands like an angel's nest,
and although he nods and bows his head
as his mother is laid to rest,
he longs to be on the silver cross
that lies on a maiden's breast.

A fortnight hence, by the river's edge,
her steps are swift and light.
"But where are my lover's eyes?" says she,
"for yours are not soft tonight."

"Farewell," says he, "my only dear,
for this is our final tryst,
and if you weep, you must weep alone,
for we must part unkissed."

She weeps, she weeps and calls after him,
but would she were alone,
for one has followed her from town
whose heart is a burning stone:

Her only sister's husband,
the herdsman Nicanor,
who's watched her from under his sullen brows
these seven years and more.

Seven long years to her sister wed,
and his thoughts are grim and dark,
for one sister's grown like a fat gray toad
but one is the morning lark.

"Let me pass, my sister's husband,
for you know we are close kin!
I cannot love my sister's man
nor lie with you in sin."
"Your love may shut me out," says he,
"but your body will let me in."

He mounts her like a battlement,
he leaves no gate untried.
The owl drifts down and swoops to find
what prey it was that cried,
and lucky the skittering tiny mouse
that knows a place to hide.

Heaven that bends above them both
is shining pure and clear.

"I shall not pray again," says she;
"for nothing up there can hear,
can see, can feel for mouse or maid
that cries aloud in fear."

"Sister, sister, draw me a bath,
for tonight I slipped and fell."
"What fall is this that has left your eyes
like the shaft of a poisoned well?"

"Sister, sister, question me not,
for a serpent has frightened me."
"What serpent is this that has left more wounds
than the wounds of Calvary?"

"Sister, the fall was your husband's fall,
the serpent Nicanor."
"A curse on your face that has tempted my man
until he could bear no more;
pray God you do not warm his seed
and banish him from our door."

He does not come for the harvest
who did such fearful sowing.
There are those who hint they know not what,
there are those who play at knowing.
But after the town wears out the tale
the seasons forget his going.

"And what shall become of my boy and me
since you've sent my man to wander?"

"We will walk and walk on the points of spears
until we've traveled yonder.

We will make our peace, as the poor must do,
for the poor have scanty choices,
and labor as one for our fatherless brood
till the choir forgets our voices,
till our feet forget the dancing floor
and our breath how the world rejoices."

Her child is meek as a small gray dove;
she asks for nothing, ever.
But she's heard of the north, where dollars grow,
and her teachers call her clever.

"Farewell, farewell, my mother, my aunt,
my cousin who guides the plow,
I go where dollars grow on trees
to pull them down somehow."
"Farewell, dear child, we have watched for you,
you must watch for your own self now."

"Fear not, my mother, my aunt," she writes,
"I am far from the honky tonks;
I have found a room like a cloistered cell
in a place they call El Bronx.

I spend my nights with an open book,
my days as a sickroom nurse.
The dollars shall be for sending home,
and the pennies for my purse."

In a Texas prison two thousand miles
from where she tends the sick,
there's a sullen man on death row
the guards call Spanish Nick

who could tell a tale, if he chose to tell,
but will soon tell nothing more,
for he's killed three men with a stolen gun
while robbing a liquor store.

In the village of San Isidro
they are gathered for a death.
The good old priest is babbling,
with every rasping breath,

of a maid alone by the river's edge
and somebody cursed by prayer,
and somebody caught like a gasping fish
in a mesh of raven hair,

and wounds unhealed as the wounds of Christ
on hands like an angel's nest,
and somebody nailed to the silver cross
that lies on a budding breast.

Woolworth

The magic is in the colors
that leap free of these
unchosen things

as the soul leaps free
of our dying,
or as poems gather their skirts

to step lightly—
looking backward, half regretful—
out of our living.

Magic surrounds
these things because they are uncramped
by our possessing.

Each is, or may be,
the untried door
beyond which everything is right:

cheap and bright, they
center a globe of light not their
own, like holy bread,

or like Voyager,
lifting away
and clear of us its magical

silver needles,
coded colors, ribbons of talk,
voices of children.

ABOUT THE AUTHOR

Rhina P. Espaillat's eighth collection of poetry, *Playing at Stillness,* won the 2003 National Poetry Book Award. Her other poetry collections include *The Shadow I Dress In,* winner of the 2003 Stanzas Prize; *Rehearsing Absence,* winner of the 2001 Richard Wilbur Award; *Where Horizons Go,* winner of the 1998 T. S. Eliot Prize; *Lapsing to Grace; The Story-teller's Hour; Rhina P. Espaillat: Greatest Hits, 1942–2001;* and *Mundo y Palabra/The World and the Word.*

Espaillat was born in the Dominican Republic and lives in Massachusetts. She writes poetry and prose both in English and in her native Spanish. Her work has been published widely in magazines and anthologies and on websites, and she has received numerous awards for her poetry. She coordinates the Newburyport Art Association Annual Poetry Contest, organizes the Powow River Poets Monthly Reading Series, and is a frequent reader, speaker, and workshop director at various schools, colleges, and cultural institutions.